# THE BLIND SIDE

By John L. Murphy

# About the Author

John Murphy and his wife Marylee have resided in Orrington, Maine since 1973. They have raised ten children, six homemade and four adopted, plus numerous foster children over the years. They have been members of East Orrington Congregational Church (EOCC) since 1985.

John is a retired professional Structural Engineer. In 1992, as EOCC was considering a new meetinghouse to replace the existing inadequate buildings, he volunteered his engineering expertise as the principal designer of the new church facility, which opened in November of 1994.

John has served on many EOCC committees, including two extended terms on the Board of Deacons. It was while on the Board of Deacons that he penned devotional essays entitled "The Deacon's Bench" for the EOCC bi-monthly newsletter, the Pen of Power.
A compilation of these newsletter essays entitled *From the Deacon's Bench* was published in 2013.

Following the onset of blindness in 2005, he was encouraged to continue writing similar essays with a focus on his experiences as a blind guy. In 2015, he published *Blindsight*, a compilation of an additional thirty of these essays. *The Blind Side* is a compilation of another thirty essays.

# Special Thanks

A very special thanks to Reverend Carl Schreiber and Reverend Doctor David Lester for encouraging and supporting this ministry of writing these essays.

I also wish to give a very special thank-you to Doctor Garth Wilbanks, MD, for many years of extraordinary eye care and for reviewing the essays contained in this book.

Also, thank-you to Amanda Goodell and Kristyn Brownell for editing and publication assistance.

# Table of Contents

# Introduction

I joined the ranks of the blind in 2005 at the age of 60. Cornea dystrophy combined with glaucoma has gradually destroyed my eyesight and significantly changed my life. I have been encouraged by many folks to record my experiences as I transitioned from sight to sightlessness.

Thus began the writing of short 400 to 500 word essays, the compilation of 30 essays into my first book entitled Blindsight, and the compilation of another 30 essays into this, my second book which I have entitled "The Blind Side".

My hope is to share, to encourage, and to inspire you, the reader, as I tell stories of my life as a blind guy.


Enjoy,

John Murphy

# 1. From The Other Side

*"And I will lead the blind in a way that they do not know, in paths that they have not known I will guide them. I will turn the darkness before them into light, the rough places into level ground. These are the things I do, and I do not forsake them." Isaiah 42:16 ESV*

As a result of two genetic eye diseases, I crossed over from my life on the visual side to the other side, the blind side, in 2005 at the age of 60. My eye diseases are Glaucoma and Fuchs Cornea Dystrophy.

Glaucoma causes an increase above normal of the internal pressure of the eye. Left untreated, the higher pressure gradually destroys the optic nerve, resulting in blindness. Glaucoma is treated with eye drops as well as a variety of surgical procedures.

Fuchs Cornea Dystrophy clouds the cornea, the clear part of the eye. Vision gradually becomes foggy and eventually there is no vision at all. The only remedy for corneal dystrophy is cornea transplant, where the diseased cornea is removed and replaced with a cornea from an organ donor.

Cornea transplants have a high degree of success for most people. There are, however, a few folks whose body rejects the transplanted cornea. I happen to be one of those few.

Unless there is an amazing technological breakthrough, I will not be returning to the visual side, and so, here I am, on the other side. My life goes on, and I have adapted well: I no longer drive a car or use power tools. I usually have an escort wherever I go. Otherwise, I do regular things, just a bit differently; and my life is pretty good.

My longtime eye care professional, Doctor Wilbanks, has made the observation that the combination of faith, family, and friends has been key to the success of my life over here on the blind side. Regarding the faith component, I often look to the encouragement and inspiration of scripture, such as Isaiah chapter 42, verse 16, which says:

> And I will lead the blind in a way that they do not know, in paths that they have not known I will guide them. I will turn the darkness before them into light, the rough places into level ground. These are the things I do, and I do not forsake them.

Yes indeed, I have been led, guided, seen things where there is no light, and found smooth pathways. I have been recording some of my experiences and reflections from over here on the other side in the context of faith, family, and friends; and I invite you, the reader, to join me as I share my blind guy essays.

It is my hope that you will spend some time looking at this glimpse into my life journey through these writings from the other side.

Enjoy.

# 2. NEW LIFE

*Forget the former things; do not dwell on the past.  See, I am doing a new thing! Now it springs up; do you not perceive it? I am making a way in the wilderness and streams in the wasteland." Isaiah 43:18,19 NIV*

Life is filled with change, both the good and the not so good, the expected and the unexpected. There are many reasons for the changes that we encounter during our life journey, such as: job or career change, marriage or divorce, financial rewards or disruption, health issues, family or community tragedy, birth or death of a family member, moving to another place, graduation or retirement.

Each change comes with a transition from the old to the new. The most dramatic change for me happened in 2005 when I lost my eyesight and began my new life as a blind person.

My old life was pretty good.  I could see.  I could do all of those things that folks with vision could do. I could see you, and I could see myself in the mirror. I could drive a car. I could see colors. I could read a book and a newspaper. I could design and build things using power tools. I could travel places by myself and be independent of others. I could see pictures.

The transition to my new life has gone well, and my new life has become pretty normal. Other than driving a car or using power tools, I do many of the things folks with vision can do. I just do them differently. I can cook, as long as the flour and sugar and other ingredients and measuring cups are in their place. I can read books, thanks to the availability of audio books. I can write essays such as this by using my computer and software for the visually impaired. I am reasonably mobile by using the tools and training provided to me.

Isaiah chapter 43, verses 18 and 19, offer some guidance on the transition from the old life to the new:

"Forget the former things; do not dwell on the past."

*These words are pretty clear. Look forward and move ahead.*

"See, I am doing a new thing! Now it springs up; do you not perceive it?"

*One needs to be cognizant of the fact that God is in charge of the new thing, and that one also needs to be perceptive of the opportunities and responsibilities that spring up in the new life.*

"I am making a way in the wilderness and streams in the wasteland."

*In spite of what may be perceived as a scary and hopeless future, as in wilderness and wasteland, there is a way forward and needs that are met along the journey of the new life.*

So, we can move ahead with confidence that the new life, whatever it may be, will work out all right.

Rejoice, and have a great day.

# 3. SENSE AND SENSE ABILITY

*"God, who began the good work within you, will continue…until it is finally finished." Philippians 1:6 NLT*

I first met Doctor Wilbanks in 1995 when he began his eye care practice in Bangor and acquired me as a patient from retiring Doctor Clark. In addition to providing quality eye care services, Doctor Wilbanks has read my church newsletter articles and my book *Blindsight*, and we often discuss them in the context of the eye care community.

Recently, I asked if he would suggest a topic that might be of interest to his patients and colleagues. He responded with the following:

"Describe how the loss of one of your principal five senses has been compensated, perhaps more than compensated, by your remaining four senses."

The principal five senses are: sight, hearing, smell, taste, and touch. As a blind guy, I do indeed use other senses to compensate for my loss of sight. But compensatory sense abilities do not just happen automatically; they are skills that are developed over time through education, training, and lots of practice.

I have had two training programs that taught me to use hearing and touch as compensatory sense abilities.

Mobility training taught me how to move about safely. I learned to feel holes, obstacles, obstructions, and surface textures with my blind guy white walking stick. During walks along the road, I stay on the gravel shoulder by feeling the different textures of grass, gravel, and pavement. The stop, look, and listen slogan for crossing a street has become stop, listen, listen, and listen some more for the all-quiet and safeness.

Computer training taught me how to use the keyboard rather than the mouse for many operations. I received training in ZoomText, a software package for the visually impaired. ZoomText enlarges and reads text that appears on my computer monitor, and while typing, it tells me the key I am using and pronounces each word when completed.

Here are a few of many other sense abilities that I have come to use:

To stay oriented as I move about my house, I listen for household noises such as fans, appliance motors, people talking, and the radio.

As I eat at the dining room table, I use the sense of touch to find cups, tableware, and my plate. With apologies to Emily Post, I use my fingers to get food onto my fork.

I have a talking clock that tells me the time or date at the press of a button.

I listen to audio books for entertainment and education.

I use stick-on tactile pads to identify buttons on the kitchen stove control panel and to identify certain keys on my computer keyboard.

My daily walk through life is missing the sight sense, but the sense abilities that I have mastered for the other senses do indeed compensate. And I am still learning new skills because God isn't finished with me, yet.

Life is good.  Have a great day.

# 4. MANIFEST

*"And as Jesus passed by, he saw a man which was blind from his birth.  And his disciples asked him, saying, 'Master, who did sin, this man, or his parents, that he was born blind?'  Jesus answered, 'Neither hath this man sinned, nor his parents: but that the works of God should be made manifest in him.'"*
*John 9:13 KJV*

The first six years of my working career were with an engineering firm in Boston, where each workday I commuted between Northern Suburbia and the City.  As each workday ended, I would leave my sixth-floor office, cross Park Square to the Trailways Bus Station, and climb aboard the big green and yellow Trombly motor coach bus for the afternoon commute home.

As I was waiting in line to board the 5:15 bus one afternoon, I observed a blind man walking toward the bus station moving his white walking stick back and forth in front of him.  He moved with purpose into the bus loading area where passengers were boarding buses for Cape Cod, New York City, Hartford, Springfield, and several communities around Boston. I was fascinated as he was the first blind man I had seen up close and in action. He moved with confidence to the end of the line of passengers boarding my bus. After I got into my seat, I watched in awe as he slowly walked down the aisle, feeling each seatback with his hand until he sensed an empty seat. He sat down in the aisle seat in front of me and the person in the window seat said "Hello George, how are you today?"

Over the next year or so, George continued to draw my attention to the ease and confidence with which he moved about in spite of being blind.

Today, as a blind guy myself, I aspire to achieve the same level of accomplishment that I so admired in George those many years ago.

John chapter 9 introduced me to another blind person. The discussion surrounding this unnamed blind man gives much inspiration to those of us who are affected by visual impairment. We are assured that our condition is not caused by anybody's sin. We also have the assurance that this condition was not a result of happenstance, but rather for the purpose that the works of God should be made manifest.

God is good.  Have a great day.

# 5. TALKIE WALKIE

*"'Master, which is the great commandment in the law?' Jesus said unto him, 'Thou shalt love the Lord thy God with all thy heart, and with all thy soul, and with all thy mind. This is the first and great commandment. And the second is like unto it, Thou shalt love thy neighbor as thyself. On these two commandments hang all the law and the prophets.'" Matthew 22:36-40 KJV*

I have been fortunate over the course of my engineering career to have worked with many outstanding engineers who have provided nurture and mentoring in the development of my own professional skills. Jack was one such engineer.

I reflect back some five decades to my very first project assignment with a Boston engineering firm. I was a new employee, just graduated from college. I was young, single, energetic, and willing to go anywhere and do anything to learn the practical applications of the Structural Engineering degree that I had recently received. I was thrilled and excited when I was assigned to a project team to survey the structural condition of a factory building in upstate New York. So off we went for a couple of weeks of field work.

The factory building that we were to inspect was one of the biggest buildings that I had ever seen. It operated 24 hours a day. The overnight shift had the least amount of noise and activity, so that was when we did our work. Because of the size of the building and the noise and production activity, the team members all had walkie talkies to communicate with one another. The project team consisted of two 3-person survey crews under the direction of Jack, the Project Engineer.

Jack was German-American. He talked with an accent and often used words and phrases that were somewhat outside the norm, and it was no surprise that Jack referred to our handheld communication devices as talkie walkies. We tried to correct him, but Jack did not budge on his seemingly incorrect word use. He said that for this project, they were talkie walkies. As the project manager, he would talk, giving instructions to the other team members. They, in turn would walk, following those instructions to do the work to accomplish the task. We successfully completed the structural survey of the building. My takeaway was the importance of clear communication and strong focus on following instructions.

Today, as a blind guy, I no longer do engineering projects such as this; but, Jack's misnomer talkie walkie is still with me, because there are instructions to give or follow in every aspect of life.

Matthew chapter 22 verses 36-40 is a talkie walkie passage: "Love the Lord thy God with all thy heart, and with all thy soul, and with all thy mind, and love thy neighbor as thyself" is the talk. Our response is the walk.

Have a great day, listen to the talk, and enjoy the walk.

# 6.  PROJECT NUMBER 2004

*"Then the King will say to those on his right, 'Come, you who are blessed by my Father; take your inheritance, the kingdom prepared for you since the creation of the world. For I was hungry and you gave me something to eat, I was thirsty and you gave me something to drink, I was a stranger and you invited me in, I needed clothes and you clothed me, I was ill and you looked after me, I was in prison and you came to visit me.'*

*Then the righteous will answer him, 'Lord, when did we see you hungry and feed you, or thirsty and give you something to drink? When did we see you a stranger and invite you in, or needing clothes and clothe you? When did we see you ill or in prison and go to visit you?*

*The King will reply, 'truly I tell you, whatever you did for one of the least of these brothers and sisters of mine, you did for me."  Matthew 25:34-40 NIV*

For most of the early years of my engineering career, I was a computer programmer for a Boston engineering firm. I worked with a team of highly intelligent and creative professionals on the cutting edge of computer applications for civil engineering.  The work was quite interesting, very challenging, enormously satisfying, and professionally rewarding.  Every pay period, I submitted my time sheet with my work hours charged to Project Number 2004.

I didn't know the name of project number 2004 until one day I came across a listing of project numbers and names.  I took a peek, expecting to see "Computer Programming" or "Research and Development".  I was dismayed to see that the name of Project Number 2004 was "Non-productive Work".

There are many behind the scenes support positions that are generally considered to be company overhead rather than revenue-producing activities, such as: reception, secretarial, accounting, custodial, and computer programming.  To label these activities as "Non-productive Work" fails to recognize the importance and vital contributions made by the folks in those positions.

In our daily walk of faith, we have neither time sheets nor project numbers, but we do have some direction for productive work. Matthew chapter 25 verses 34-40 is one such example. These verses give us guidelines for interaction with others along our faith journey.

When somebody says to us, or when we say to somebody else, words such as: I was hungry and you gave me something to eat; or, I was thirsty and you gave me something to drink; or, I was a stranger and you invited me in; or, I needed clothes and you clothed me; or, I was ill and you looked after me; or, I was in prison and you came to visit me – then we know that productive work is happening, because God has said: "whatever you did for one of the least of these brothers and sisters of mine, you did for me."

Have a joyful and productive day.

# 7. DOWN THE DRAIN

*"If we confess our sins, he is faithful and just to forgive us our sins, and to cleanse us from all unrighteousness."*
*1 John 1:9 KJV*

Several years ago, before the onset of blindness caused by glaucoma and cornea disease, I was invited to speak to an audience of young children at a career day function to discuss my work as an Engineer with the City of Bangor wastewater collection and treatment system.

At the appointed time, I arrived with my props. I had: two 3-liter clear plastic bottles, one containing fresh water, and one empty, and I had a number of small soda bottles, each containing a sample from liquids collected from around the house. I had: somebody's cold morning coffee, some milk with Cheerios floating in it, some dirty dishwater from the kitchen sink, some bathwater from the tub, some laundry water from the washing machine, some leftover tomato soup from last night's supper, some pancake batter, some orange juice, and a few other samples of household liquids that come from our normal daily activities.

The presentation began with a question: "Where did your Cheerios and milk go that you did not finish at breakfast this morning?" With a bit of prompting, the children answered: "down the drain", and I emptied the small bottle with the milk and Cheerios into the large empty bottle. And so it went with each small bottle of various household liquids.

"Where does it go?"

The children all answered, "down the drain", and another something was added to the big bottle. When I was finished, the small bottles were empty, and the big bottle was nearly full of the mixture of liquids that represent the stuff that goes down the drain every day.

Then, comparing the two large bottles, one with the yucky, sticky, soapy, brownish liquid, and one with the clean water, I explained that my job involved collecting the yucky stuff that goes down the drain and transforming it into clean water. I then asked them what their life would be like if all of this yucky stuff did not go down the drain but just stayed around. Some of the answers I heard were sour milk, rotten food, and stinky smells. The children all agreed that when it all goes down the drain, life is cleaner, healthier, and much better.

Our daily activities produce things other than what we send down the drain. Every day we use phrases such as: "put it in the trash", "send it to recycling", "add it to the compost pile", and, "burn it"; And because these things happen, life is cleaner, healthier, and much better.

We also have 1 John chapter 1 verse 9, which tells us that if we confess our sins, he is faithful and just to forgive us our sins, and to cleanse us from all unrighteousness. And again, because this happens, life is cleaner, healthier, and much better.

Yes indeed, life is good. Rejoice, and have a great day.

# 8. In My Garden

*"They sowed fields and planted
vineyards that yielded a fruitful harvest."
Psalm 107:37 NIV*

Maine singer-songwriter David Mallett wrote "The Garden Song" in 1975, and over the ensuing years, the song has been performed by artists in many music genres, including: folk, country, children's, and Celtic. A song about gardens is a nice addition to the mix of things we gardeners do in the late Spring.

As I began to work in my garden, the weather was sunny and warm, the birds were singing, a breeze kept the bugs away, and my hopes for a good crop were very much in tune with Psalm chapter 107 verse 37.

This will be the fourth year that I have had a garden since I joined the ranks of the blind. This year I will grow: green and yellow string beans, cucumbers, squash, and garlic. My blind guy garden consists of four raised bed spaces in my back yard. The garden is set up for gardening by touch.

The wood enclosures define the spaces, which are about six feet wide and of varying lengths. I prepare the soil by pulling out the plants from the garden of last year and picking out the rocks that appeared over the winter. Then I use my hands and a small hand rake to mix the soil with organic compost. Then I form hills across the width of the garden. The seeds are planted at the top of the hills. I then know that any plants that grow in the valleys and on the sides of the hills are weeds.

I harvest by feeling the string beans and following the vines for cucumbers and squash. And as I spend time in my garden, I hear in my mind the catchy tune and lyrics of "The Garden Song":


Inch by inch, row by row,
gonna make this garden grow.
All it takes is a rake and a hoe
and a piece of fertile ground.

Inch by inch, row by row,

someone bless these seeds I sow,
someone warm them from below,
till the rain comes tumblin' down.

Pullin' weeds and pickin' stones,
man is made of dreams and bones.
Feel the need to grow my own,
cause the time is close at hand.

Grain for grain, sun and rain,
find my way in nature's chain.
Tune my body and my brain
to the music from the land.

Plant your rows straight and long,
temper them with prayer and song.
Mother Earth will make you strong
if you give her love and care.

Old crow watchin' hungrily,
from his perch in yonder tree.
In my garden I'm as free
as that feathered thief up there.

I enjoy working in my garden. I use
the opportunity to soak up some
sunshine, to listen to the birds perform
nature's symphony, and to commune
with God. And I enjoy "The Garden

Song".  It says much about being in my garden.

Have a great summer, and may your garden yield a fruitful harvest.

# 9. Cucurbita

*"Now he who supplies seed to the sower and bread for food will also supply and increase your store of seed and will enlarge the harvest of your righteousness."* 2 Corinthians 9:10 NIV

Cucurbita is not one of my invented words. It is a Latin term for the family of plants that includes gourds, squash, and pumpkins. Pumpkins are a big part of our late autumn tradition. We carve Jack-O-Lanterns for Halloween and make pumpkin pies for Thanksgiving.

For the two big pumpkins that we had this year, I had the task of removing the seeds from the inside of the pumpkins. So, along with making the Jack-O-Lanterns and the pies, I had two dishes full of seeds. There seemed to be a lot of seeds, and my curiosity compelled me to count them. We retired folks sometimes do strange things for our edification.

There were 795 seeds from one pumpkin and 737 seeds in the other one. I find it interesting that one seed produced enough pumpkin for several pumpkin pies, and the potential for more than 700 pumpkin plants in the next growing season. If I were to plant all of these seeds and had one pumpkin from each seed, I would have a really great harvest of these orange things from the Cucurbita family.

I am reminded of the message of 2 Corinthians chapter 9 verse 10, which tells us that he who supplies seed to the sower and bread for food will also supply and increase your store of seed and will enlarge the harvest of your righteousness. This righteousness is that which comes from God, as we are told in Romans chapter 3 verse 22: "This righteousness is given through faith in Jesus Christ to all who believe".

We know from the parable of the sower in Matthew chapter 13 verses 19 through 23 that the seed is the Word of God, and that there are four responses to the sowing of the seed:

Response 1: "When anyone hears the message about the kingdom and does not understand it, the evil one comes and snatches away what was sown in their heart. This is the seed sown along the path."

Response 2: "The seed falling on rocky ground refers to someone who hears the word and at once receives it with joy. But since they have no root, they last only a short time. When trouble or persecution comes because of the word, they quickly fall away."

Response 3: "The seed falling among the thorns refers to someone who hears the word, but the worries of this life and the deceitfulness of wealth choke the word, making it unfruitful."

Response 4: "The seed falling on good soil refers to someone who hears the word and understands it. This is the one who produces a crop, yielding a hundred, sixty or thirty times what was sown."

All gardens need to be weeded, even spiritual gardens. We know from 1 John chapter 1 verse 9 that if we confess our sins, he is faithful and just to forgive us our sins, and to cleanse us from all unrighteousness. The confession and forgiveness of our known sins and God's cleansing of the unknown ones removes the weeds and other obstacles that impede our hearing and understanding of God's word.

We know from Galatians chapter 5 verses 22 and 23 that the fruit of the Spirit is: love, joy, peace, patience, kindness, goodness, faithfulness, gentleness, and self-control.  This is the harvest of our righteousness.

2 Corinthians chapter 9 verse 10 promises us that we will have this harvest enlarged, and that we will have an increased store of seeds for sowing love, joy, peace, patience, kindness, goodness, faithfulness, gentleness, and self-control.

Have a great day, and may you be productive in God's word.

# 10. PICKER-UPPER

*"And my God will supply every need of yours according to his riches in glory in Christ Jesus." Philippians 4:19 ESV*

In the fall of 1982, I was briefly out of work.  For an interim job, I accepted an offer to be an apple picker at a local orchard. On the first day of harvest, the picking crew was given a brief training session on the protocols of apple picking. We were taught to carefully handle each apple as bruised apples were unacceptable for sale in grocery stores. We were taught how to use the triangular shaped ladders to get up into the tree.

We were taught to gently grasp the apple and to twist it to free it from the tree. We were taught to carefully place each apple into the canvas bag that we wore at our waist. We were taught how to empty full bags into boxes. We were paid for each box that we filled. Drops - apples on the ground - were often bruised and could not be placed in our boxes. So, I was an apple picker for seven weeks. I earned about $100 per week and could take home a bag of drops every day.

Today, I only pick apples from the tree in my front yard. I have not forgotten the techniques that I learned and applied way back then. But my blind guy apple picking techniques are a bit different. I walk down to my tree using step count and my walking stick. I know I am near the tree when I step on apples that have fallen to the ground. Then I reach overhead with my walking stick and whack the branches that I can reach, knocking off a few more apples that have not been blown off by the wind. Then I get down on my knees, lay my walking stick flat on the ground, and sweep the walking stick across the ground, locating the drops. I feel the apples with my fingers, and place the firm ones in a grocery bag. Once I have picked a bagful of apples, I go back to the house and get out my apple peeling gizmo. I put an apple on the device, turn the crank, rotating the apple and moving it through the cutting assembly which peels, cores, and slices the apple. Tis pretty neat, and, the apples are soon ready for applesauce and apple pie.

Each apple season, I am reminded of those days so many years ago when I picked apples for a period of time. I am also reminded of the message of Philippians chapter 4 verse 19. I was out of work and was provided a job. I was hungry and was given a big bag of apples every day. Today, as a blind guy, I have been supplied with the resources to go about my life, which includes being an apple picker. Or, more appropriately, an apple picker-upper.

Life is good. Smile, rejoice, and give thanks.

# 11. Proficiency

*All Scripture is God-breathed and is useful for teaching, rebuking, correcting, and training in righteousness, so that you, a man of God, may be thoroughly equipped for every good work.*
*2 Timothy 3: 16, 17 NIV*

According to the dictionary, if you have proficiency with something, you are pretty good at it. As I was listening to 13-year-old Austin and six-year-old Jakob playing the other day, I overheard Jakob say, "Hey Austin, let's keep doing this until we get it right". Those few words reminded me of a long-ago time when I was ten and brother Eddie was eight. Dad was a carpenter working on a new house next to where we lived in Hampden. At the end of the workday, Eddie and I went over to see the construction progress and to raid the pile of scrap wood that was accumulating at the site. Dad bought us some tools, taught us the fundamentals of using them, and told us to have fun making things with the scrap pieces of wood.

So, we learned how to use a hammer and a saw. We learned to use a hand drill to make holes in the wood. We learned how to use a coping saw to make things with curves. We learned how to use a six-foot long folding ruler and learned early on to measure twice and cut once. We learned how to use a screwdriver, and soon knew the difference between a Phillips and a flat screwdriver. We learned about nuts and bolts and pliers and wrenches.

And so, we made things from scrap wood, and in the process, we bent nails, pounded our thumbs, cut our fingers, got pinched with the pliers, and got splinters in our hands. But we learned how to use tools and how to build things of our own creation. And we got pretty good at it.

As I got older and my vision began to fail, I had new skills to learn and new tools to use to function in a life of blindness. I gained proficiency with these new tools and skills in the same way that I did with the hammer, saw, and the other tools those many years ago.

Our spiritual walk is similar.  2 Timothy chapter 3, verses 16 and 17 gives us the process.  All scripture is God-breathed and is useful for teaching, rebuking, correcting, and training in righteousness, so that you, a man of God, may be thoroughly equipped for every good work.

Whether: tools, sports, job skills, marriage, raising children, understanding scripture, algebra homework, or other, the learning process is the same.  We are taught, we make mistakes, we correct our mistakes, and we practice, practice, and practice some more until we are pretty good at it.  That's proficiency.

So, let's remember the words of little Jakob and keep doing whatever we are doing until we get it right.  Smile, be joyful, and have a great day.

# 12. LOSTNESS

*Or suppose a woman has ten silver coins and loses one. Doesn't she light a lamp, sweep the house and search carefully until she finds it?  And when she finds it, she calls her friends and neighbors together and says, 'Rejoice with me; I have found my lost coin.' In the same way, I tell you, there is rejoicing in the presence of the angels of God over one sinner who repents.*
*Luke 15:8-10 NIV*

Not so long ago, my daughter Erin was looking through one of my photo albums and saw that I had been a paperboy as a youngster.  Yes, indeed, I was a paperboy, delivering the Bangor Daily News in East Hampden where I lived at the time. Back in the late 1950s, the Bangor Daily News cost 7 cents a day, 42 cents per week per customer. At the end of the week, the 42 cents collected from each of my 80 customers added up to $33.60, of which $8.00 was my weekly pay.

One memorable event in my paperboy career occurred on a winter day on the school playground. While playing at recess, my wallet containing the week's collection money fell out of my pocket and disappeared somewhere in those acres of snow.

For me, a 12-year-old paperboy, there was no rejoicing that day. The loss of more than four weeks of pay and the need to raid my savings for $25.60 to pay my Bangor Daily News supervisor were not reasons for joyfulness. However, I did learn the valuable lesson of paying extra attention to things of importance.

Today, I am one of those things of importance. Being blind, I need to be especially vigilant about where I am, and to be constantly aware of my surroundings for personal safety and to avoid lostness.

Lostness is perhaps a new word, but to me, it means the condition of being completely disoriented, like wearing a blindfold and not knowing which way to turn and needing help from others to get reoriented. Lostness also is the spiritual condition of being disoriented with God, and when one recognizes the lostness and asks God for help to get reoriented, there is rejoicing by those of Luke chapter 15 verse 10.

Back to the lost wallet full of money - after diligent searching when the snow melted in the Spring, I found it.

Rejoice with me, for God is good.

# 13.  TESTED

*Every test that you have experienced is the kind that normally comes to people. But God keeps his promise, and he will not allow you to be tested beyond your power to remain firm; at the time you are put to the test, he will give you the strength to endure it, and so provide you with a way out. 1 Corinthians 10:13 GNT*

Don and I were best friends as youngsters.  We rode bikes, went fishing and water skiing in the summer, went sliding and tobogganing in winter, delivered newspapers, ran on the Hampden Academy cross-country team, and lived in the same rooming house in the Boston area on our first career jobs.

Behind Don's childhood home were acres of fields and woods. When we were about thirteen, we pretended to be explorers as we prowled Don's backyard wilderness. One day, we discovered an old flatbed truck body that had been abandoned near the edge of the woods. We asked Don's dad if we could use the old truck body for the floor of a cabin for camping out on warm summer nights. He gave us his permission and also contributed some old scrap building materials. So, we built the one-room cabin and moved in, along with Cindy, Don's big brown Chesapeake Bay Retriever dog.

Late one night, Cindy growled and woke us up, alerting us that something was outside the cabin. We got out of our sleeping bags and grabbed our flashlights to investigate. Right outside our full-length screen door was a skunk. Cindy barked, the skunk sprayed, and we thought for sure we were going to die. The skunk scurried away, and we dashed out of the cabin gasping for fresh air. Then, in the dark of the night, we trudged the half mile back to Don's house to wake up his parents to ask what to do after being sprayed by a skunk.

Unbeknownst to us at the time, we had just experienced the promise of 1 Corinthians chapter 10 verse 13: "Every test that you have experienced is the kind that normally comes to people."

Perhaps we were being tested for wilderness coping skills, such as dealing with being sprayed by a skunk. But God keeps his promise, and he will not allow you to be tested beyond your power to remain firm. We survived the most terribly awful experience we two young boys had ever had. "At the time you are put to the test, he will give you the strength to endure it, and so provide you with a way out." We indeed did endure, and went on to learn that tomato juice and canned tomatoes are an effective remedy for neutralizing skunk odor.

As I reflect back on this very memorable incident, I have the assurance and the confidence that no test, not skunk nor blindness, will exceed my ability to withstand, and that each test will have a sound solution.

Rejoice, and have a great day.

# 14. Bean Boozled

*Taste and see that the LORD is good! How blessed is the person who trusts in him! Psalm 34:8 ISV*

The dictionary says bean boozle means that a joke has been played on you. I was bean boozled a few days after Christmas of 2016 when we went to visit with our son Mike and his family in suburban Syracuse. We had a few days to visit with Mike, Lori, twin five-year-old grandsons Collin and Garrett, and with three-week-old grandson Elliott.

The twins had a new game to play with me called Bean Boozled. The game is played with jelly-beans of ten different colors. There are two jelly-beans for each color, outwardly identical but with significantly different flavors. Here are the colors and flavors:

White: Spoiled Milk or Coconut

Yellow: rotten egg or buttered popcorn

Orange: Barf or Peach
Light Green: Booger or Juicy Pear
Rainbow:  Stinky Socks or Tutifruti
Tan:  Dead  Fish  or  Strawberry Smoothie
Blue: Toothpaste or Blueberry
Brown:  Canned  Dogfood  or Chocolate Pudding
Gold:  Moldy  Cheese  or  Caramel Corn
Green: Lawn Clippings or Lime

This is how we played the game. One of the twins spun the spinner. When the spinner stopped, it pointed to one of the ten colors. The other twin and I each picked up one of the jelly-beans of that color. Then the fun began.

On the count of three, each player bit into his jelly-bean. The player with the good-flavored jelly-bean was the winner. The player with the bad flavored jelly-bean, usually me, was Bean Boozled. The howls of laughter from Collin and Garrett told me that I had the appropriate reaction when I lost. We had a lot of fun using our sense of taste.

Taste is one of the five senses. The others are sight, smell, sound, and touch. I am missing the sight sense, and therefore rely on these other senses to compensate. The game that I played with the twins reminds me of our spice shelf, where there are eight outwardly identical spice containers, each with a different spice. The spices are: ground pepper, pepper corns, cinnamon, garlic powder, onion powder, salt, chicken bouillon cubes, and beef bouillon cubes. I can identify the pepper corns and bullion by sound when I shake the container. To differentiate the like-sounding bouillon cubes, I left half of the top seal of the beef flavor to identify the container by touch. The pepper, cinnamon, and garlic have easily identifiable smells. The salt and onion powder are identified by taste. And so, even without sight, I can pick the right spices when cooking.

Back to taste, Psalm chapter 34 verse 8 reminds us to: "Taste, and see that the LORD is good!" This taste test is different from the game I played with the twins in that there is no bad taste and no one is Bean Boozled. Yes indeed, God

is good, all the time.  Have a great day,
and may your life be blessed.

# 15. WALKWAYS

*For we are his workmanship, created in Christ Jesus for good works, which God prepared beforehand, that we should walk in them.  Ephesians 2:10 ESV*

In March of 2017, Marylee and I went to Colorado for a visit with our son Joshua and his wife Amanda, and their two boys Jarod and Kaladin.  We were excited about the visit, and were looking forward to celebrating Jarod's 7th birthday, and to meeting 15-month-old Kaladin for the first time.

Kaladin was not yet walking, but was right on the verge of doing so. He crawled around the house at warp speed, and could take a few baby-steps before falling.  We were wondering if he would achieve the significant milestone of beginning to walk before our visit was over.  So, while playing with the little guy, I began to think of the many words that we use to describe walking, that action of moving about by placing one foot ahead of the other in anticipation of achieving a desired goal. Consider, for example, the following and the subtle differences in meaning as words are substituted for walk: I walk to the store, or, I dash to the store, or, I hike to the store, or, I limp to the store, or, I saunter to the store.

I found many of these words, and I began to compile a list I call walkways, which currently looks like this:

Amble, baby-step, backstep, bolt, burst, careen, climb, clog, clomp, crawl, creep, dance, dart, dash, drift, flee, flounder, gambol, gimp, glide, hike, hobble, hop, hustle, jog, jump, limp, lope, lumber, lurch, march, mosey, pace, pad, parade, plod, prance, promenade, prowl, race, ramble, roam, run, sashay, saunter, scamper, scurry, shuffle, sidestep, skip, slide, slip, slosh, sneak, snowshoe, somnambulate, sprint, stagger, stalk, stampede, step, stomp, stride, stroll, strut, stumble, swagger, tiptoe, traipse, tread, trek, trot, trudge, waddle, wade, waltz, and wander.

'Tis hard to believe there are so many walkway words. But there are more, because there is another aspect of the word walk: that of providing guidance. For example: she walked the elderly man to his seat.

Walkways for this type of walk include: accompany, chaperone, escort, guide, lead, shepherd, and usher.

In pondering Ephesians chapter 2 verse 10: "For we are his workmanship, created in Christ Jesus for good works, which God prepared beforehand, that we should walk in them," we have the promise of walking, or ambling, or running, or skipping, or waltzing, or staggering, or stumbling, or escorting, or shepherding in the good works that God has provided.

Regarding Kaladin and his walking progress, a few days after we returned home, Amanda reported that Kaladin had indeed started walking. He crawled to the toy box, found Jarod's toy plastic baseball bat, stood up, and started walking like me, his blind grandfather, moving the toy bat in front of him to search for obstacles in his path of travel.

Life is good.  Have a great day, and enjoy your walk and the many walkway variations.

57

# 16. BLINDWALKER

*"For we walk by faith, not by sight". 2 Corinthians 5:7 KJV*

*For now we see in a mirror dimly, but then face to face. Now I know in part; then I shall know fully, even as I have been fully known. So now faith, hope, and love abide, these three; but the greatest of these is love. 1 Corinthians 13: 12, 13 ESV*

Blindwalker is one of those words that I invent when an existing word fails to adequately capture my thoughts. I define Blindwalker in three ways:

Blindwalker 1 is Me. I am a blind guy who walks, who stands up and takes the action of moving about by placing one foot ahead of the other in anticipation of achieving a desired goal. I became a Blindwalker 1 in early 2005. I have a changed life, as I now do most things differently and some things not at all. I am doing well as a Blindwalker 1 and find every day to be cherished.

Blindwalker 2 is you. You HAVE VISION and are willing and ready to be a walker of the blind. You escort me, the blind one, arm in arm from one place to another place SAFELY AND WITHOUT INCIDENT, and you do much more. You say hello, introduce yourself, give me a firm handshake or a hug. You get me coffee AND FOOD at get-togethers. You place the pen point on the line for my signature. You clean up the spills and messy countertop from my cooking. You drive me places for meetings and appointments and to visits with grandchildren that I have never seen. You provide me with audio books to "READ" and you discuss with me the books that you are "reading". You read my mail to me and help pay my bills. You read my essays and offer comments and encouragement. You are my family, friends, work colleagues and health care professionals who fulfill this important role of Blindwalker 2s. You are special to me, and I give you my sincere thanks.

Blindwalker 3 is both you and me. We are described by 2 Corinthians chapter 5 verse 7: "For we walk by faith, not by sight." We understand that the spiritual side of our life journey often involves the unseen. We understand that we are a work in progress as described in 1 Corinthians chapter 13 verse 12: "For now we see in a mirror dimly, but then face to face. Now I know in part; then I shall know fully, even as I have been fully known." We know from 1 Corinthians chapter 13 verse 13 that we have three powerful tools to use as Blindwalker 3s: "So now faith, hope, and love abide, these three; but the greatest of these is love."

As we journey through our life as Blindwalker 3s, may strong faith, never-ending hope, and God's unconditional love shine brightly.

Smile, rejoice, cherish the walk, and have a great day.

# 17. LINES

*Whom shall he teach knowledge? and whom shall he make to understand doctrine? them that are weaned from the milk, and drawn from the breasts. For precept must be upon precept, precept upon precept; line upon line, line upon line; here a little, and there a little. Isaiah 28:9,10 KJV*

I like to walk laps around the building we call East Orrington Congregational Church, using the parking lots and drives that surround the facility. I have found that this is a safe place to do walks without being concerned about cars, curbs, and potholes. Each lap includes both level areas and gentle slopes. I paced the distance around the building at one-eighth of a mile. My usual goal is to do sixteen laps, a two-mile walk.

Although I am a blind guy, I do have some very limited vision, and I am able to faintly see the white lines painted on the parking lots. So, I use the lined areas to help me stay oriented and on course. I use the cross-hatched lines at the rear walkways to verify my location as I circle the building. I use the curved lines at the corners of the parking areas to know when to change direction. I use the yellow line at the front door of the church to mark the start and finish of each lap.

During one of my recent walks, passing line after line in the parking lot, I recalled a verse of scripture that I had learned a long time ago that described spiritual growth as a line upon line building process. I couldn't remember the exact reference, so, when I had the opportunity, I looked it up and found that it was Isaiah chapter 28, verses 9 and 10.

I can sense a correlation here between my physical walk and my spiritual walk.

My physical walk is a step by step, lap-by-lap process toward a goal such as the sixteen lap, two-mile walk.

My spiritual walk is similar. The step-by-step process is the intake by reading or hearing, and study of God's Word, line upon line, precept upon precept, a little here and there, with the goal of building up increasing amounts of spiritual knowledge and doctrinal understanding.

Have a great day, and enjoy your walks, step-by-step and line-by-line.

# 18. DOODLES

*His divine power has given us everything we need for a godly life through our knowledge of him who called us by his own glory and goodness. Through these he has given us his very great and precious promises, so that through them you may participate in the divine nature, having escaped the corruption in the world caused by evil desires. For this very reason, make every effort to add to your faith goodness; and to goodness, knowledge; and to knowledge, self-control; and to self-control, perseverance; and to perseverance, godliness; and to godliness, mutual affection; and to mutual affection, love. For if you possess these qualities in increasing measure, they will keep you from being ineffective and unproductive in your knowledge of our Lord Jesus Christ. But whoever does not have them is nearsighted and blind, forgetting that they have been cleansed from their past sins.*
*2 Peter 1:3-9. NIV*

I have always liked to doodle, drawing sketches of my ideas as I try to get a bunch of thoughts to gel into a solution or explanation for whatever I happened to be working on at the time. I still doodle as a blind guy, although without the sketches. I use my computer that is equipped with software that reads to me those words that I type or download. Then I doodle around with the words and ideas. Sometimes I come up with some interesting conclusions. For example, after spending a bunch of time with 2 Peter chapter 1, my doodles brought me to the conclusion that building a Godly Life has many similarities to building a house. Here are my doodle thoughts:

Project:  Building a Godly Life.

Purpose: Participation in the divine nature.

Cost of materials:  Free.

Source of Materials:  God.

Sequence of Construction:  Faith, goodness, knowledge, self-control, perseverance, Godliness, mutual affection, and love. The foundation is Faith and the roof is Love.

Energy Source:  God's divine power through knowledge of His very great and precious promises.

Maintenance / Improvement Requirements:  All items in increasing measure, similar to Isaiah 28, line upon line, precept upon precept, a little here, a little there.

Consequence of Neglect:  being ineffective and unproductive in the knowledge of Jesus Christ.

Consequence of Inaction:  No Godly Life, Spiritual Blindness.

God has given us everything we need to build, maintain, and improve the Godly life that He wants us to have.

Have a great day, and enjoy your Godly-life gift.

# 19. THANKSGIVINGNESS

*Give thanks in all circumstances; for this is God's will for you in Christ Jesus.*
*1 Thessalonians 5:18  NIV*

I am often asked to write about Murphy's Law, which says "If anything can go wrong, it will." We all experience things going wrong in our life journey. Some are serious matters and some are not. Here are a few of my more humorous encounters with Murphy's Law that I call 'oops incidents':

Not so long ago, I made Marylee a cup of coffee. I overlooked the critical step of adding coffee to the coffee maker filter. Oops.

Similarly, I made grandson Austin a cup of hot chocolate without adding the packet of cocoa... oops... and there is the tea with no tea bag.  Oops.

One day we decided to have hamburgers for supper. I retrieved a package of burger from the freezer and thawed it, only to discover that it was mincemeat. Oops.

For Christmas, I was given some new boots. As I was struggling to get them on, I was informed that I was trying to put them on the wrong feet. Oops.

I wore a new shirt to church one Sunday. A lady in the pew behind me said: "nice new shirt John," as she peeled a sticker tag off my shirt collar. Oops.

With the chicken in the crock pot, I put the potatoes in the oven to bake. An hour later, I went to get the potatoes for supper and discovered that I had forgotten to start the oven. Oops.

I made mac and cheese for lunch one day. When it was time to add the powdered cheese, I mistakenly grabbed a packet of hot chocolate. Oops.

I picked up a bag of trail mix and started munching. It tasted really awful so I asked Marylee what I was eating. It was cat treats. Oops.

OK, so maybe my blindness is an excuse for such oopsiness, but I was doing such oopsy things before I lost my eyesight.

While driving one August day, I was stopped by a policeman. The issue was an inspection sticker that had expired in August… of the previous year. Oops.

The one really memorable incident of oopsiness was the day I left my car parked on the street behind my office at Bangor City Hall with the engine running for about three hours. Oops.

Yes indeed, things do go wrong, and for many reasons other than oopsiness. The degree of wrongness may often be much more serious than those Murphy's Law encounters listed above, such as a house fire or unexpected death of a family member or a serious car accident or financial issues or health concerns.

In all such incidents of things going wrong, 1 Thessalonians chapter 5 verse 18 reminds us that our response is to be thankful. So, let us rejoice, even in the things that go wrong, and be in a state of thanksgivingness in all circumstances.

# 20. FLAVESCENT

*No one has ever seen God; but if we love one another, God lives in us and his love is made complete in us. 1 John 4:12 NIV*

Everybody knows that the grass is green, the sky is blue, fire trucks are red, school buses are yellow, UPS trucks are brown, and oranges are, well, orange. Bad guys wear black, good guys wear white, and Kings wear purple. Children learn the colors of the rainbow at an early age, and remember the name Roy G. Biv, the acronym for Red, Orange, Yellow, Green, Blue, Indigo, and Violet.

My computer printer has four colors of ink. From the red, blue, yellow, and black, the printer can combine the inks to produce any color, such as crimson, goldenrod, mauve, turquoise, and flavescent. In case you are wondering, flavescent is a real word that means yellowish or turning yellow, perhaps like the birch trees in October.

I see few colors nowadays. I see dark, light, orange, and yellow, and, at some point in the future, I will see no colors at all.  I am fortunate that my loss of vision occurred later in life, and I can remember what colors look like, but, I have often wondered how to describe colors to someone who has been blind from birth, one who has never seen colors before.  How does one describe "red" in words?  Or "yellow"?  Or any other color?  What about shades of color? Or fluorescence?  Or dullness or brightness or  shininess?  Color is only known by the visual sense.

Color cannot be determined by smell or hearing or touching or tasting.  Colors exist, even if they cannot be seen or described with words.  For those of us who cannot see colors, we accept by faith that the sky is blue and the grass is green and so on. In like fashion, no one has ever seen God in His fullness and glory. But like the colors that the blind one cannot see, He indeed exists as is manifested by the love that is made complete and shared by those who understand and believe.

Have a great day, and cherish the colors.

# 21. Bread

*But he answered and said, It is written, Man shall not live by bread alone, but by every word that proceedeth out of the mouth of God. Matthew 4:4 KJV*

I frequently make bread, a task that I can do really well as a blind guy. Today I made dinner rolls to go with our chicken soup evening meal. The bread recipe is easy to remember: half cup of sugar, three tablespoons of yeast, two teaspoons of salt, two and one-half cups of warm water, one egg, half cup of vegetable oil, and five cups of flour. I mix the ingredients using the mixer with the bread hook attachment and let the dough rise until the mixing bowl is full. I then place the dough onto the bread board and prepare it for baking. This recipe will make two loaves of bread, or two pans of dinner rolls, or four pizza crusts.

Bread provides nourishment and is considered a basic food staple. Bread is often used as a symbol of our daily food requirements. Bread also provides livelihood for many folks, such as: bakers, delivery drivers, and storekeepers.

As I make bread, I often recall Matthew chapter 4 verse 4: "Man shall not live by bread alone, but by every word that proceedeth out of the mouth of God." Regarding this, I have several favorite passages, such as Psalm chapter 23, 1 John chapter 1, John chapter 6, Galatians chapter 5, and especially Isaiah chapter 55 beginning with verse 6:

> Seek the LORD while he may be found; call on him while he is near. Let the wicked forsake their ways and the unrighteous their thoughts. Let them turn to the LORD, and he will have mercy on them, and to our God, for he will freely pardon.
>
> For my thoughts are not your thoughts, neither are your ways my ways, declares the LORD. As the heavens are higher than the earth, so are

my ways higher than your ways and my thoughts than your thoughts.

As the rain and the snow come down from heaven, and do not return to it without watering the earth and making it bud and flourish, so that it yields seed for the sower and bread for the eater, so is my word that goes out from my mouth: It will not return to me empty, but will accomplish what I desire and achieve the purpose for which I sent it. You will go out in joy and be led forth in peace; the mountains and hills will burst into song before you, and all the trees of the field will clap their hands. Instead of the thorn bush will grow the juniper, and instead of briers the myrtle will grow. This will be for the LORD's renown, for an everlasting sign that will endure forever.

Let us always remember that Man shall not live by bread alone, but by every word that proceedeth out of the mouth of God. Rejoice, and have a great day.

# 22.  GOOD GRIEF

*Through him we have also obtained access by faith into this grace in which we stand, and we rejoice in hope of the glory of God.  Not only that, but we rejoice in our sufferings, knowing that suffering produces perseverance, and perseverance produces character, and character produces hope.*

*Romans 5:2-5.  ESV*

I wonder how many of you subconsciously added the words Charlie Brown to the title of this writing. The expression "Good grief" is frequently associated with one of my favorite comic strip characters, Charlie Brown.

As a blind guy, I haven't seen a Peanuts comic strip for a long time, but there are many things that I remember about Charlie Brown: I remember that Charlie Brown likes to fly kites, but his kite always gets tangled up in the kite-eating tree; he likes to kick the football, but Lucy always moves the football out of the way and Charlie Brown falls flat on his back; Charlie Brown likes to play baseball, but he never wins a game;  he gets a lump of coal in his mailbox for Valentine's Day;  his Christmas tree leaves much to be desired;  and, his reaction is often "Good Grief", an expression that means unbelievable, shocking, something that is hard to imagine.

We all have Charlie Brown experiences where life deals us the unexpected, where we have to face disappointment, loss, or change, and where our initial reaction is, perhaps, "Good grief, I can't believe this is happening to me." At such times, we find ourselves in a process called grief, defined as the normal and natural emotional reaction to loss or change of any kind. Grief has long been recognized as having five stages: denial, anger, bargaining, depression and acceptance. But what comes after reaching the acceptance stage of the grief process?

As I reflect back on those days when I could see to read comic strips, I can picture in my mind Charlie Brown as an example of what to do next. He gets back up on his feet and tries again, with the kite, the football, the baseball, the mailbox, and the Christmas tree. Charlie Brown does not give up. He gets up and moves forward with his life. Charlie Brown demonstrates those traits of perseverance, character, and hope found in Romans chapter 5. And as Romans chapter 5 tells us, let us rejoice, even in our Charlie Brown experiences.

Smile, and have a great day.

# 23. PERSPICACITY

*For the Lord gives wisdom; from his mouth come knowledge and understanding. Proverbs 2:6 NIV*

When I read a book, essay, article, or other writing, I like to understand the words that I encounter. For example, the definitions of the key words of Proverbs chapter 2 verse 6 are as follows: Knowledge is facts, information, and skills acquired by a person through experience or education. Understanding is the mental or intellectual comprehension and the thorough familiarity with that knowledge. Wisdom is the ability to use knowledge and experience to make good decisions and judgments.

Have you heard the word perspicacity before? For those of you who know that I sometimes invent a word to illustrate a topic, I assure you that this is not one that I invented. I learned perspicacity a long time ago, probably from one of my friends who was into vocabulary development. Perspicacity is defined as the ability to understand things quickly and make accurate judgments. It combines in one word the essence of knowledge, understanding, and wisdom.

As my life transitioned from sight to sightlessness, perspicacity should have been an operative word. Yes, I quickly gained the knowledge and understanding about Glaucoma and Fuch's Corneal Dystrophy, but when I learned that the likely outcome for me was blindness, the good judgment part of perspicacity was replaced with denial.

Denial said I need not be concerned because science and technology would find a cure. I drove my car, used power tools, crossed streets, and travelled alone when good judgment said not to do those things. But eventually, good judgment did prevail as I came to realize that I needed to be positive and pro-active in my approach to visual impairment. So, I did the mobility training and the computer training and the other trainings to acquire the skills that blind folks use to get along. And, other than not being able to drive my car or use power tools, I get along quite well.

Proverbs chapter 2 verse 6 tells us of three gifts from God.  God gives us knowledge of Himself.  God gives us the ability to understand that knowledge.  God gives us the wisdom to use that knowledge and understanding.  In summary, it can be said that God gives us perspicacity, the ability to understand things quickly and make accurate judgments.

May these gifts be a part of your life journey today.

# 24. Amazing Grace

*Therefore, since we have been justified by faith, we have peace with God through our Lord Jesus Christ.*

*Through him we have also obtained access by faith into this grace in which we stand, and we rejoice in hope of the glory of God.  Romans 5: 1,2. ESV*

In 1975, Marylee and I volunteered to host a refugee family from Vietnam in our Orrington home.  The family, residing in a refugee camp until a host family could be found, consisted of a mother and six children, ages 6, 8, 12, 14, 16, and 18.

We were 20-somethings with three young children of our own, and we faced questions about our sanity and our emotional, physical, and financial ability to undertake this venture, but we were confident in our belief that God's amazing grace was sufficient.  We moved forward with preparations to welcome this family into our home, perhaps providing them with a glimmer of hope as they began life anew in a strange land.

And some amazing things began to happen: small amounts of money showed up in the mail and by personal gifts, we received a total of $122 and some change; a summer camp that was closing donated three sets of bunk beds; a local church cancelled a rummage sale and gave us everything, correctly trusting that some things would be suitable for the family; an area church women's group donated sheets, pillowcases, and blankets.

Following their arrival in September of 1975, we took the family to a shoe store to replace the flip-flops they had on their feet. The total cost for seven pairs of shoes was exactly the $122 plus change that we had received from donations. A gentleman came to our home one day with bicycles for the children. One man volunteered to give the family a ride to church every Sunday. An elderly lady donated $5 a month from her Social Security, hoping this donation would be enough for her to meet the family in person. This was gladly arranged with a Vietnamese dinner and evening visit. Many folks left fresh garden produce at our door during harvest season.

As winter approached and after much searching, we found a snowsuit to fit 12-year-old Ngoc. The cost was $25. Shortly after returning home from purchasing the snowsuit, a group of Orrington Rainbow Girls knocked at our door and presented us with $25 that they had collected in a fundraiser service project.

The school-teachers and staff were truly awesome as they welcomed the Vietnamese children into the classrooms, even though they spoke little or no English. The family lived with us for eight months, with such happenings as described above occurring frequently. Amazing Grace. Today, they live in California as successful Americans and as a very real part of our extended family. Romans chapter 5 verse 2 tells us that we stand in Grace.

Rejoice and be thankful, for Amazing Grace surrounds us.

# 25.  DESCRIPTIVENESS

*Lord, who may dwell in your sacred tent? Who may live on your holy mountain?  The one whose walk is blameless, who does what is righteous, who speaks the truth from their heart; whose tongue utters no slander, who does no wrong to a neighbor, and casts no slur on others;  who despises a vile person but honors those who fear the Lord;  who keeps an oath even when it hurts, and does not change their mind; who lends money to the poor without interest;  who does not accept a bribe against the innocent.  Whoever does these things will never be shaken.*
*Psalm 15:1-4  NIV*

Descriptiveness is not one of my invented words.  According to the dictionary, descriptiveness means: "to characterize by description."  After living with us for about ten years, Hooch passed away in the Summer of 2018. Hooch was an eighty pound, mostly Norwegian Ridgeback, family dog. Hooch joined our family after I lost my eyesight, so I can say that I never actually saw him.  But, I can describe his qualities. He was: gentle, protective, friendly, and totally devoted to his master, our son Adam.

I am reminded of the following example of descriptiveness sent to me some time ago entitled Inner Strength:

> If you can start the day without caffeine, if you can get going without pep pills, if you can always be cheerful, ignoring aches and pains, if you can resist complaining and boring people with your troubles, if you can eat the same food every day and be grateful for it, if you can understand when your loved ones are too busy to give you any time, if you can take criticism and blame without resentment, if you can ignore a friend's limited education and never correct him, if you can resist treating a rich friend better than a poor friend, if you can conquer tension without medical help, if you

can relax without liquor, if you can sleep without the aid of drugs, ...Then you are probably the family dog!

Yes indeed, these words describe Hooch, and they also describe qualities that we might like to have for ourselves. But there are other qualities that are also important for us, such as those found in Psalm chapter 15.

If we aspire to attain these qualities, folks may very well be saying about each of us these words of descriptiveness: Your walk is blameless; you do what is righteous; you speak the truth from your heart; your tongue utters no slander; you do no wrong to a neighbor; you cast no slur on others; you despise a vile person but honor those who fear the Lord; you keep an oath even when it hurts; and do not change your mind; you loan money to the poor without interest; you do not accept a bribe against the innocent. You do these things and are not shaken.

May Psalm chapter 15 be a guiding light for all of us. Smile, rejoice, and have a great day.

# 26. TODAY

*"This is the day that the Lord has made; let us rejoice and be glad in it."*
*Psalm 118:24  ESV*

As I began writing this essay near the end of May of 2019, I could say with assurance that today was a beautiful day. The sun was shining brightly, warming both my back and the soil as I prepared my blind guy garden boxes for planting the new crop of green and yellow string beans.

I was told that the sky was brilliant blue, that the grass was beginning to turn green, that the trees had leaves on them, and that the dandelions were in bloom. I heard robins and cardinals and sparrows and finches serenading me from the treetops. I heard crows and blue jays, each making their unique sound that I frequently call a "joyful noise." I heard the chatter of a squirrel as he was probably raiding the backyard bird feeder. There was a gentle breeze that was keeping the black flies and mosquitos at bay. Yes, indeed, today was truly a beautiful day. I found myself repeating the words of Psalm chapter 118 verse 24: "This is the day that the Lord has made; let us rejoice and be glad in it".

And then, in the midst of joy and gladness, I recalled yesterday.

Yesterday it rained all day for the second or third day in a row. The black flies and mosquitos made it unbearable to be outside. The birds seemed to be subdued in their singing. During the previous night, a strong gust of wind had toppled a tree in our back yard. I was experiencing some discomfort from a recent eye procedure, and my joints were aching from the damp weather.

In my state of blindness, I was bumping into door frames and furniture more frequently than usual. Marylee was suggesting that I was being a bit of a grouch and that perhaps I should "get myself right with God." OK. I know how to do this. Recognition plus acknowledgement equals restoration.

On that day, I obviously needed some help from Marylee to recognize that I was not in tune with God.  I paused for a moment, took a few deep breaths, and acknowledged that I had overlooked the fact that Psalm chapter 118 verse 24 also applies to the not so beautiful days as well as the really good ones.

I should have been joyful and glad in spite of all of those discomforts. I should not have been such a grouch.  I needed to be mindful that every day is from God and is to be met with rejoicing and gladness; And so, with the recognition and acknowledgement of my shortcomings, I claimed the promise of restoration of being in tune with God; and I was prepared to begin today as I enthusiastically embraced that today is the day that the Lord has made.

Have a great day, be joyful and glad, today and every day.

# 27. Anxiousness

*Do not be anxious about anything, but in every situation, by prayer and petition, with thanksgiving, present your requests to God.  And the peace of God, which transcends all understanding, will guard your hearts and your minds in Christ Jesus.*
*Philippians 4: 6,7  NIV*

One of my favorite Irish funnies goes something like this:

Paddy was driving down the street in a sweat because he had an important meeting and couldn't find a parking place. Looking up to heaven, he said, "Lord, take pity on me. If you find me a parking place, I will go to church every Sunday for the rest of me life and give up me Irish whisky." Miraculously, a parking place appeared.

Paddy looked up again and said, "Lord, never mind, I found one."

'Tis indeed a funny story, and I hope it gave you a chuckle. In the beginning of the story, Paddy had a serious case of anxiousness. Anxiousness is not one of my invented words. It is a real word that means a state of being anxious.

The dictionary defines anxiousness as "experiencing worry, unease, or nervousness, typically about an imminent event or something with an uncertain outcome."

Synonyms for anxious include: Afraid, Agitated, Apprehensive, Bothered, Concerned, Disquieted, Distressed, Disturbed, Edgy, Fearful, Fretful, Jumpy, Nervous, Overwrought, Perturbed, Stressed, Tense, Troubled, Uneasy, and Worried.

So, Paddy was experiencing anxiousness, as we all do from time to time. For me, the blind guy, I find that I have anxiousness about: curbs and holes when I walk; about falling down stairs; about missing the chair when sitting; about sitting in somebody's lap; about slipping on the ice; falling and about getting disoriented in an unfamiliar place; about bumping into someone and knocking them down; about tipping over the display case where I get my hair cut; about encountering an electric car while crossing the street; about bumping into a restaurant waiter with a fully loaded carrying tray; about being all alone in a busy, crowded, noisy place; about tripping over the family dog or other unseen objects; and the list goes on.

I need not dwell on my anxiousness. I can claim the promise of Philippians chapter 4 verses 6 and 7: "Do not be anxious" (or afraid, agitated, apprehensive, bothered, concerned, disquieted, distressed, disturbed, edgy, fearful, fretful, jumpy, nervous, overwrought, perturbed, stressed, tense, troubled, uneasy, or worried) "about anything" (this means what it says, anything and everything) "but in every situation, by prayer and petition, with thanksgiving, present your requests to God." This is how to address anxiousness.  Paddy had it wrong when he tried to make a deal with God.

"And the peace of God, which transcends all understanding, will guard your hearts and your minds in Christ Jesus" (this is God's answer to anxiousness, a promise that is for all of us).

Rejoice with me, be always thankful, and have a great day.

# 28. In Darkness

*When Jesus spoke again to the people, he said, "I am the light of the world. Whoever follows me will never walk in darkness, but will have the light of life." John 8:12  NIV*

*"The light shines in the darkness, and the darkness has not overcome it."  John 1:5 NIV*

There are many examples of what it means to be in darkness. In darkness can mean being out at night rather than during the day. In darkness can mean a power outage with no lights, heat, or communications. In darkness can mean being ignorant about a subject rather than being knowledgeable and proficient. In darkness can mean being sad or grieving rather than being joyous. In darkness can mean being left out of some activity. In darkness can mean being in an illegal or bad situation. In darkness can mean being associated with Satanic or evil activity. In darkness can mean being without the presence or fellowship of God. In darkness can mean being blind.

As I write this essay in the early days of 2020, I reflect back over my years of being in darkness, of being blind. For many years beginning in the early 1990s, I had very gradual loss of vision. In early 2005, my vision had declined such that it became unsafe for me to drive my car. I handed over the car keys to Marylee and have since used that point of time as the beginning of my Life of Blindness.

At that time in early 2005, I could still see most things. I told folks that my vision was on a giant dimmer switch that moved one click toward dark every day. So, here I am some fifteen years later. I still have a tiny bit of vision left. I can still distinguish light from dark, I can still see some motion and shadows, and, although most colors have long since disappeared, I can still see yellow and orange under certain conditions.

I have had fifteen years of preparation for that future time when the light sensitivity will be gone, the dimmer switch will reach its final click, and I will be left in total and complete darkness. The thought of being in total and complete darkness is scary, and does cause me some degree of anxiousness, but, I have many promises from scripture that provide encouragement and hope, such as John chapter 8 verse 12, and John chapter 1 verse 5.

John 8:12 says: "Jesus spoke again to the people, he said, "I am the light of the world. Whoever follows me will never walk in darkness, but will have the light of life."

John 1:5 says: "The light shines in the darkness, and the darkness has not overcome it." I take great comfort in knowing that no matter what form of darkness envelops me, the light of life shines brightly, and always will.

Rejoice with me, be always thankful, and have a great day.

# 29. A Choice of Two

*Get rid of all bitterness, rage, anger, harsh words, and slander, as well as all types of evil behavior.  Instead, be kind to each other, tenderhearted, forgiving one another, just as God through Christ has forgiven you. Ephesians 4:31,32*


*You, my brothers and sisters, were called to be free. But do not use your freedom to indulge the flesh; rather, serve one another humbly in love.  For the entire law is fulfilled in keeping this one command: Love your neighbor as yourself.*
*Galatians 5:13, 14 NIV*


For many years in my career as a civil engineer, up until blindness interfered, I had the privilege and honor of being on the speaker's circuit.  I travelled far and wide to tell others in the water quality profession about the interesting things that we were doing in the Bangor area. My style of speaking was to begin each presentation with something humorous that was related to the subject at hand, as I will do now.

So, did you know that there are three kinds of people in the world? There are those who can count, and those who can't. I hope you smiled at this. Now, on to the more serious material.

An audio book that I recently heard had a sub-theme that most decisions come down to a choice of two. Do I stay up late to complete my algebra homework? Yes or no. When I reach the end of the road, which direction do I turn? Left or right. If I turn the faucet lever toward the left, what water temperature will I get? Hot or cold. When I flip a coin, what face will be on top? Heads or tails.

In our walk of faith, we frequently encounter situations where we face a similar choice of two. For example, Ephesians chapter 4 verses 31 and 32 offer choices in two categories in answer to the question: "How should I behave?"

Choice 1: bitterness, rage, anger, harsh words, and slander, as well as all types of evil behavior.

Choice 2: Kindness to each other, tenderhearted, forgiving one another, just as God through Christ has forgiven you.

Similarly, Galatians chapter 5 verses 13 and 14 have choices in two categories regarding our call to be free and how we should respond.

Choice 1: Use your freedom to indulge the flesh.

Choice 2: Serve one another humbly in love. For the entire law is fulfilled in keeping this one command: "Love your neighbor as yourself."

The words to love your neighbor come from the great commandment of Matthew chapter 22, which says: "Love the Lord thy God with all thy heart, and with all thy soul, and with all thy mind, and love thy neighbor as thyself."

The choice of two here is implied.

Choice 1: Ignore the commandment.

Choice 2:  Follow the commandment.

May we all choose to follow the commandment and love one another. Rejoice, be thankful, and have a great, love-filled day.

# 30.  RUN THE RACE

*And let us run with endurance the race that is set before us.  Hebrews 12:1 ESV*

*And I will lead the blind in a way that they do not know, in paths that they have not known I will guide them. I will turn the darkness before them into light, the rough places into level ground. These are the things I do, and I do not forsake them.  Isaiah 42:16 ESV*

Many years ago, when I was a high school student at Hampden Academy, I was a runner on the cross country team.  I have many memories from those days of long ago:

I remember that cross country courses were about 2.5 miles long and included fields, woods, hills, and level ground. I remember that we ran a 2.5 mile practice every day, and had competitions with other area high schools twice each week during the fall sports season. I remember that distance running was rigorous, demanding, and physically exhausting.

I remember Coach Hutchins, affectionately known by all as Hutch. Hutch was a very inspirational teacher and coach, and often challenged and motivated us to do more than we thought we could do. I remember that after running our 2.5 mile practice one day, Hutch challenged us to run the course again. I remember that as we ran the 2.5 miles for the second time that day, we did not fully understand nor appreciate that Hutch was encouraging us to stretch our level of endurance and become better runners. I remember that we did indeed become better runners and went on to win the league championship.

Today, some six decades later, my raceway is a treadmill with the course measured in number of steps rather than miles. Recently, as I approached my 2000 step treadmill goal, I remembered the challenge of Hutch those many years ago. I decided to run the course again, and I did it, doing another 2000 steps.

The race that is set before me nowadays is my life journey going forward. As in my high school cross country days, the race before me may be rigorous, demanding, and physically exhausting. As with the treadmill, the raceway may be entirely different from the expected. I may at times be called upon to put forth extra effort, to run the course again. I can expect to encounter an interesting array of challenges, opportunities, and possibilities every day, and, even though I am blind, both physically and otherwise, Isaiah chapter 42 verse 16 assures me that I can indeed run the race set before me:

> I will lead the blind in a way that they do not know, in paths that they have not known I will guide them. I will turn the darkness before them into light, the rough places into level ground. These are the things I do, and I do not forsake them.

Have a great day, and may you run well the race that is set before you.

www.ingramcontent.com/pod-product-compliance
Lightning Source LLC
Chambersburg PA
CBHW021112130726
47988CB00003B/988